KINDERGARTEN

By: Sue Laroy and Ken Carder
Illustrations: Mike Johnson, Jeffrey McCormack and Dave Billman
Cover Illustration: Tammy Ortner

Credits:
Publisher: Twin Sisters Productions, LLC
Executive Producers: Kim Mitzo Thompson, Karen Mitzo Hilderbrand
Music by: Kim Mitzo Thompson, Karen Mitzo Hilderbrand, and Hal Wright,
except *The Animal Alphabet,* words by Nancy Wright, and *The ABC Song.*
Music Arranged by: Hal Wright
Workbook Authors: Sue Laroy, Ken Carder
Book Design: Angelee Randlett, Christine Della Penna

This edition published by School Specialty Publishing,
a member of the School Specialty Family.

Send inquiries to:
School Specialty Publishing
8720 Orion Place
Columbus, Ohio 43240-2111

1 2 3 4 5 6 7 8 9 10 TWNS 09 08 07 06 05

ISBN 0-7696-4453-8

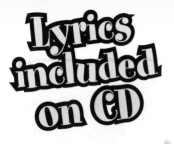

Acrobat Reader 6.0.1 system requirements

WINDOWS
- Intel® Pentium® processor
- Microsoft® Windows 98 Second Edition, Windows Millennium Edition, Windows NT® 4.0 with Service Pack 6, Windows 2000 with Service Pack 2, Windows XP Professional or Home Edition, Windows XP Tablet PC Edition
- 32MB of RAM (64MB recommended)
- 60MB of available hard-disk space
- Internet Explorer 5.01, 5.5, 6.0, or 6.1

MACINTOSH OS X v.10.2.2-10.3
- PowerPC® G3 processor
- Mac OS X v.10.2.2-10.3
- 32MB of RAM with virtual memory on (64MB recommended)
- 70MB of available hard-disk space

Acrobat Reader 5.1 system requirements

MACINTOSH OS 9.1-10.2.1
- PowerPC processor
- Mac OS 9.1, 9.2, or 9.2.2, or Mac OS X v.10.1.3, 10.1.5, or 10.2
- 64MB of RAM
- 30MB of available hard disk space (an additional 60 MB is needed temporarily during installation)
- HFS formatted hard drive
- Additional 70 MB of hard-disk space for Asian fonts (optional)
- Web browser support
- The Web browsers within which Adobe PDF files may be viewed are:
  Internet Explorer 5.0
  Netscape Navigator 4.5 to 4.77, 6.1
  America Online 6.0

Adobe Acrobat Reader Installation Instructions

WINDOWS
1. Insert CD into Drive.
2. Access CD by double-clicking "My Computer" on the desktop.
3. Open "PC Installer" folder.
4. Double-click "AdbeRdr60_enu_full.exe"
5. Follow Installation Instructions.

MACINTOSH OS X v.10.2.2-10.3
1. Insert CD into Drive.
2. Double-click on "PDF and Installers" Icon on the desktop.
3. Open "MAC Installer" folder.
4. Open "MacOS 10.2.2-10.3" folder.
5. Drag "Adobe Reader 6.0" folder to your hard drive.

MACINTOSH OS 9.1-10.2.1 (Acrobat Reader 5.1)
1. Insert CD into Drive.
2. Double-click on "PDF and Installers" Icon on the desktop.
3. Open "MAC Installer" folder.
4. Open "MacOS 9.1-10.2.1" folder.
5. Double-click on "Acrobat Reader Installer."
6. Click "Continue" when prompted.
7. Follow installation instructions.

The Animal Alphabet

Name: _____

- -

_____

A is for
Alligator
not making a sound.

B is for
Bumblebee
buzzing all around.

C is for a
caterpillar
crawling by.

D is for the
Duck
trying to fly.

E is for an **Elephant** making a wish!

F is for one fancy **Fish.**

G is for **Grasshopper** — look at him hop!

H is for the **Horse** trying to stop!

I is for an **Insect** with six long legs.

J is for the **Jaguar** looking for eggs.

K is for the **Kangaroo** king.

L is for **Lion** who is trying to sing.

6

M is for a
a quiet little
Mouse.

N is for
Night crawler
crawling to his house.

O is for the
wise, old
Owl.

P is for
the **Pig**
trying hard to growl.

7

Q is for the sleeping **Quail.**

R is for **Rabbit** reading her mail.

S is for **Salamander** — isn't he silly?

T is for the **Turtle** whose name is Willy!

U
is for
Unicorn
with her shiny horn.

V
is for
Vulture
who is eating the corn.

W
is for the Worm
that wiggles out of sight.

X
is for
X-ray fish
that swims all night.

© 2006 Twin Sisters IP, LLC. All Rights Reserved.

Y

is for the

Yellow Jacket

looking at you.

Z

is for the **Zebra**

that lives in the zoo.

Now I Know My
Animal Alphabet!

ABCDEF
GHIJKLM
NOPQRST
UVWXYZ

Word Families

Write the missing beginning letter for each word in the following word families. Talk about which letters stay the same in each word and how those common letters make these words a family. Use the picture as a clue for each word.

_at   _en

_at   _en

_at   _en

Word Families

Write the missing beginning letter for each word in the following word families. Talk about which letters stay the same in each word and how those common letters make these words a family. Use the picture as a clue for each word.

_an   _an

_an   _og

_og   _og

Ending Sounds

Say the name of the picture. Circle the **ending letter** sound you hear.

b t p	z f p
r s v	g h j
k r n	t m g

Learning to Count

Circle the Amount

Identify and trace the number at the beginning of each row.
Circle the amount of objects that represents that number.

Circle the Amount

Identify and trace the number at the beginning of each row.
Circle the amount of objects that represents that number.

Learning to Count

Write the Number

Write the number that represents the amount of objects shown.

WHAT NUMBERS ARE MISSING?

Write the number that comes next.

Write the number that comes first.

1, 2, ___

5, 6, ___

9, 10, ___

10, 11, ___

___, 13, 14

___, 6, 7

___, 10, 11

___, 18, 19

Learning Colors, Shapes, and Sizes

What Size Is It?

This activity demonstrates the concept that things come in different sizes. Talk about the different sizes of other things. Are you taller or shorter than your child? Is a tree larger or smaller than a flower? Are your shoes longer or shorter than your child's?

LARGER or SMALLER?

Circle the object in each pair that is larger.

TALLER or SHORTER?

Circle the object in each pair that is shorter.

Colors,
colors

everywhere
—on the ground and in the ai

Sing along with Track No. 5,
Look Up High, Look Down Low.

Colors, colors!
Blue I see

flowers,

birds,

the deep blue sea.

Colors, colors!
Red I see

apples,

cherries,

strawberries.

Colors, colors!

Yellow I see

lemons,

ducks,

and
bumblebees.

Colors, colors!

Green I see

bugs

and leaves,

and yummy peas.

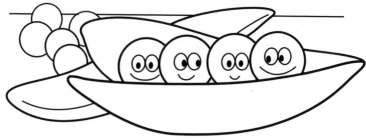

Colors, colors!

Orange

I see

goldfish,

pumpkins,

carrots to eat.

25

Colors, colors!
Purple I see

plums

and grapes,

violets for me.

Color Learning Activities

Scratch Painting

Cover a piece of paper with different colors of paint in a random design. When the paint is dry, cover the paper with black crayon. Use a coin to scratch off the crayon, drawing a picture or making a design and revealing the colors below.

Green Food Day

Once a week have a color-coordinated food day. On Green Food Day, for example, decide how you would like to include the color green in your breakfast, lunch, or dinner. Here are some ideas:

- Wear something green
- Sit on green grass, carpet, towel, bed sheet or green old tablecloth.
- Put together snacks for the picnic that are green: green grapes, celery, pickles, and green apples.

Ask your child what his favorite green food is and why. How many green things can you think of together? Make a list.

The Rainbow Game

During short drives around town or longer road trips, call out a color and have your kindergartner search for something of that color. What colors are the most difficult to find? What colors are the easiest to find?

Sorting by Color

This is a great way to get your child involved in helping with the laundry, while reinforcing color skills. Lay out construction paper in several colors on a table. As you fold the laundry, ask your child to sort the laundry by color and stack it next to the appropriate color. Did you use all of the colors? Did you have some laundry left over, that didn't match any of the colors?

Play and sing along with *What Color Are You Wearing?* (track 4), *Look Up High, Look Down Low* (track 5), and *Jump Rope Rhyme* (track 6) on the accompanying CD.

Marble Paint

Pour several colors of acrylic paint into individual containers. Drop a few marbles into each container and mix until the marbles are completely covered with paint. Place a piece of paper into a shoebox or plastic storage container. Spoon the marbles onto the paper. Pick up the box or container and move the marbles around to create an abstract masterpiece. Spoon the marbles out of the box.

Eat a Shape

Reinforce shape recognition with this fun and yummy activity. Make your favorite sugar cookie recipe. Roll out the dough. Use inexpensive cookie cutters or a knife to cut the dough into squares, rectangles, triangles, and other shapes. Bake the cookies. To further reinforce the identification of the shape, have your child ice the cookies, paying attention to how the shape is formed. When the cookies are finished, call out a shape and have your child find that shape and then eat that shape!

Use inexpensive cookie cutters or a knife to cut a variety of shapes out of slices of sandwich meat, cheese, and bread. For example, make a heart-shaped sandwich of meat, cheese, and bread; a square-shaped peanut butter and jelly sandwich. When the sandwich is made, eat the shape!

Shapely Designs

Cut sponges into the common shapes—square, circle, rectangle, and triangle. Dip the sponges into acrylic paint and press on a large piece of construction paper or poster board. Make several designs by arranging and/or overlapping the shapes. Talk about the characteristics of each shape as you work together.

Color and Shape Twister

Cut out circles, squares, triangles, rectangles, stars, hearts, and other shapes from large pieces of colored construction paper. Place the shapes randomly on the floor. Ask your child to hop on the green square or place his hand on the yellow circle or kneel on the red triangle.

Start slowly and increase the speed gradually. Play this game with other family members and your child's friends, too.

Shape Hunt

Look for shapes you see throughout your daily routine. Point out circle plates, rectangle trucks, square televisions, octagon stop signs, diamond kites, stars on signs, etc. Play "I Spy" by saying, for example, "I spy a red rectangle." Sing *Where Is That Shape?* from the accompanying CD.

Kitchen Ceramics

Give your child some flour in a small mixing pan and pour water while he/she kneads it into dough. Together make balls and various shapes. Use triangle-, circle-, heart-, square-, and diamond-shaped cookie cutters. Talk about the characteristics of each shape as you work together. Put these shapes in a hot oven to harden. Later, once cooled decorate the shapes with paint.

Five- and Six-Year-Old Kindergarten Skills

Use the following list of skills and benchmarks as a guide to assess your Kindergartner's abilities and academic progress.

A Kindergartner should be learning to:

READING and WRITING

- Enjoy reading alone, with, and to others
- Communicate thoughts and feelings about a story
- Identify repetition, rhythm, rhyming patterns
- Identify a specific part of a story
- Identify and discuss characters
- Predict events using picture cues
- Illustrate, act out, and retell a story
- Understand that letters are symbols that represent sounds and several letters together may make a word
- Match letters to sounds
- Identify the initial consonant of a word
- Make pictures or words that begin with the same sound
- Combine some letters to represent words
- Show that words may be combined to create sentences
- Demonstrate some conventions of print, including top to bottom, left to right, and letter formation
- Trace lines and shapes top to bottom, left to right
- Write story drafts using invented spellings

Learning Colors, Shapes, and Sizes

Five- and Six-Year-Old Kindergarten Skills

Use the following list of skills and benchmarks as a guide to assess your Kindergartner's abilities and academic progress.

A Kindergartner should be learning to:

MATHEMATICS

- Count to 100 by ones, fives, and tens
- Match numbers to a set of objects, up to 20
- Identify common shapes and solids
- Compare objects of different lengths, weights, and volumes
- Continue a pattern
- Recognize days of the week, months, seasons, and understand use of a calendar

SCIENCE

- Ask "What if?" and "Why?" questions
- Describe observations made with all five senses
- Observe and describe seasonal patterns, cycles
- Describe animals' similarities, differences, behavior, changes